THE FUNNIEST SPACE JOKE BOOK EVER

Collect them all!

THE FUNNIEST SPACE JOKE BOOK EVER

By Joe King

Illustrated by Nigel Baines

Andersen Press

First published in 2017 by
Andersen Press Limited
20 Vauxhall Bridge Road
London SW1V 2SA
www.andersenpress.co.uk

2 4 6 8 10 9 7 5 3 1

British Library Cataloguing in Publication Data
available.

ISBN 978 1 78344 503 5

Printed and bound in Great Britain by Clays Limited,
Bungay, Suffolk, NR35 1ED

Awesome Astronauts

What's an astronaut's favourite chocolate?

A Mars bar

What TV channel do astronauts like to watch?

The comet-y channel

What's an astronaut's favourite snack?

Astro-nuts

Can't you eat nuts like a normal person?

How do astronauts add more protein to their diet?

They make it meteor

How do you get a baby astronaut to go to sleep?

You rocket

Where would an astronaut park his space ship?

Next to a parking meteor

How do astronauts serve dinner?

On flying saucers

How do astronauts serve drinks?

In sunglasses

What is an astronaut's favourite drink?

Gravi-tea

What is fast, loud and crunchy?

A rocket chip

How does an astronaut describe her job?

Heavenly

How do astronauts say sorry?

They Apollo-gise

Where do astronauts keep their sandwiches?

In a launch box

5

What do you call a bonkers spaceman?

An astro-nut

How do spacemen pass the time on long trips?

They play astronauts and crosses

What did the astronaut say when he left Earth?

To infinity and beyond

What did the astronaut call her baby?

Interstellar

Two astronauts are about to go on a spacewalk. It's the first time for one of them, so he confesses that he's nervous and asks how the other astronaut keeps calm under the pressure of everything that could go wrong. The experienced astronaut says, 'I don't feel any pressure out there.'

What is an astronaut's favourite key on the keyboard?

The space bar

Why is an astronaut like an American football player?

They both want touchdowns

Why don't astronauts get hungry after being blasted into space?

Because they've just had a big launch

8

What did the astronaut wear to keep warm?

Apollover

Why are astronauts successful people?

Because they always go up in the world

What do astronauts wear to bed?

Space jammies

Why did the astronauts leave the space bar?

Because there was no atmosphere

What do astronauts do when they get angry?

Blast off

What do you call an astronaut that answers back?

A sass-tronaut

If athletes get athlete's foot, what do astronauts get?

Missile-toe

First astronaut: I'm hungry
Second astronaut: So am I, it must be launch time!

What's an astronaut's favourite kind of salad?

Rocket

Why don't astronauts relate well to other people?

They're not always down-to-Earth

**What did the baby astronaut
want to do when she grew up?**

Reach for the stars

**What do you do if you
see a space man?**

Park in it, man

**Did you hear about the
astronaut who broke the law
of gravity? She got a
suspended sentence.**

Planetary Punchlines

Why was the Earth offended?
Because it kept getting mooned

13

What did Earth say to the other planets?

'You guys have no life!'

Which planet in the solar system did the aliens crash-land on?

Splaturn

How does the Earth get clean?

It takes a meteor shower

Why did the planet join the solar system?

It always wanted a son

How do you organise a space party?

You planet

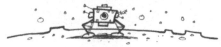

Why do the other planets hate the sun?

Because everything revolves around it

What's purple and floats in space?

Planet of the grapes

What did the planet say to the astronaut?

Nothing – planets can't talk

What songs do planets sing?

Nep-tunes

What do planets like to read?

Comet books

What planet has the best TV?

Nep-toons

I think that's called a full moon!

How does Jupiter hold up his trousers?

With an asteroid belt

What do astronauts call Saturn?

The undefeated solar system hula hoop champion

Why did Mickey Mouse go to space?

To find Pluto

What did Mars say to Saturn?

'Give me a ring some time!'

**What did the doctor
say to Earth?**

*'I'm afraid you've got a
case of the humans.'*

Who is the most famous pop star in space?

Freddie Mercury

What did the planet say to the asteroid?

'Comet me, bro!'

While living on Earth might be a little expensive, at least you get a free trip around the sun every year.

Where do comedians come from?

Planet of the japes

Night-sky Nonsense

Why is the moon bald?

He has no 'air

How many balls of string would it take to reach the moon?

One. A very large one.

When do you know the moon has had enough to eat?

When it's full

What holds the moon up?

Moonbeams

Why couldn't the astronaut book a room on the moon?

Because it was full

What do you call a parasite on the moon?

A lunar tick

How does the man in the moon get his haircut?

Eclipse it

Sun: Why do you get up so late?

Moon: It's just a phase I'm going through

Why did the cow want to go to space?

Because she wanted to go to the mooooooon

**Why did the cow
jump over the moon?**

*Because the farmer's
hands were cold*

Knock, knock
Who's there?
Luke
Luke who?
Luke up and see the moon

**What do moon people do
when they get married?**

They go off on their honeyearth

**Why does a moon rock taste
better than an Earth rock?**

Because it's a little meteor

24

Are the moon and the Earth good friends?

Yes, they've been going around together for years

What kind of light goes around the Earth?

A satel-light

Explorer 1: Hey, the Northern
Lights are out!
Explorer 2: Well, go and fix them!

**Why do some stars
wear sunglasses?**

Because they're movie stars

**What do you call two stars
having a fight?**
Star wars

Why did the star get arrested?

Because it was a shooting star

**Why didn't the Dog Star
get the joke?**

He was too Sirius

Why didn't the sun go to university?

*Because it already had
a million degrees*

What kinds of fish
live in space?
Starfish

Why did the sun go to school?
To get brighter

If there was no such thing as night, the sun would run out twice as fast.

Did you hear about the man who stayed up all night looking for the sun to come up?
Yes, it finally dawned on him

Galactic Giggles

What did the meteorite say when it landed?

'I think I just hit rock bottom.'

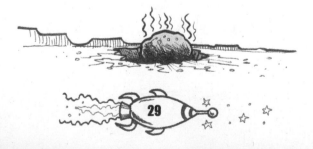

**What do you call a
wizard in space?**

A flying saucer-er

**I'd tell you a space joke but
it's too out of this world.**

Which *Star Wars* character works at a restaurant?

Darth Waiter

Why is there no air in space?

Because the Milky Way would go off

What do you call Chewbacca when he has chocolate stuck in his fur?

Chocolate chip Wookiee

How many ears does Captain Kirk have?

A left ear, a right ear, and a final frontier

This is Cat and Fiddle to Mission Control... we are over the moon!

Why did the cow go to outer space?

To visit the Milky Way

What kind of saddle do you put on a space horse?

A saddle-lite

Why did Anakin Skywalker cross the road?

To get to the dark side

32

Why do Daleks eat apples?

*Because an apple a day
keeps the Doctor away*

**What do black holes talk
about to each other?**

Dark matters

I would go to space, but the
cost is astronomical.

Where does Buzz Lightyear go on holiday?

Infinity and beyond

What vehicle does a T-Rex use to go from planet to planet?

A dinosaucer

**What do you call a
nervous Jedi?**

Panicking Skywalker

**If a rock that hits a planet
is a meteorite, what do we
call the ones that miss?**

Meteowrongs

**What kind of cars do
Jedis drive?**

To Yodas

**Why is the Millennium
Falcon so slow?**

*Because it takes a millennium
for it to get anywhere*

Knock, knock
Who's there?
Doctor
Doctor who?

Why did the baby go to outer space?
To visit the Milky Way

Which programme do Jedis use to open computer files?
Adobe Wan Kenobi

What do you call Wall-E's cousin who cleans the floor?

Floor-E

What does Doctor Who eat with spaghetti?

Dalek bread

What do you call a doctor in the sewers?

Doctor Poo

Why is Yoda such a good gardener?

Because he has green fingers

Who is the scariest Time Lord?

Doctor Boo

What did the Dalek say when he broke up with his girlfriend?

Ex-terminate

Knock, knock
Who's there?
Art
Art who?
R2-D2

What do you call a time-travelling cow?

Doctor Moo

Alien Antics

What do you call an alien with three eyes?

An Aliiien

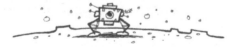

What is an alien's favourite type of sweets?

Martian-mallows

I do like Christmas!

Why did the alien knit itself three socks?

Because it grew another foot

Where do aliens go to school?

Universe-ities

What did the alien confess to the astronaut?

'I use to be addicted to time travel, but that's all in the past now.'

What do you call a spaceship that drips water?

A crying saucer

What do aliens cook on the barbecue?

Unidentified frying objects

Why was the alien green?

She hadn't taken her space sickness pills

How do aliens keep themselves clean?

They have a meteor shower

What makes more noise than an alien?

Two aliens

Why are aliens forgetful?

Because everything goes in one ear and out three others

Why did the stupid alien get so excited after he finished his jigsaw puzzle in only six months?

Because on the box it said, 'From 2 – 4 years'

First alien: Stand still, there's something ugly on your shoulder!
Second alien: What is it?
First alien: Your head!

What kind of cartoons do aliens watch?

Lunar-toons

What does E.T. do when he gets homesick?

He phones home

How do you greet a three-headed alien?

Hello, hello, hello

What do you call an alien wearing earmuffs?

Anything you like – he can't hear you

What do aliens study in music class?

The big band theory

What did the alien say to the garden?

Take me to your weeder

What is big, yellow and prickly, has three eyes and eats rocks?

A big, yellow, prickly three-eyed alien whose favourite food is rocks

What did the alien grandparent say to his grandchildren?

'Live long and prosper.'

What do you get if you cross Santa Claus with a space ship?

A U-F-Ho-ho-ho

What did the alien say when she came home from work?

'I'm all spaced out.'

What did the alien say when he landed on Earth?

'I need some space.'

Why didn't the alien get burned when it went to the sun?

It went at night

Why do aliens make crop circles?

Because they're corny

Scientific
Side-
Splitters

**What's an astronomer's
favourite snack?**
Hubble-gum

Why is the law of gravity useful?

Because if you drop something, it's much easier to get it off the floor than off the ceiling

How does Einstein begin a story?

'Once upon a space-time. . .'

Scientist: Please help me, doctor,
I keep seeing into the future.
*Doctor: I see. And when
did this start?*
Scientist: Next Tuesday
afternoon.

When does time travel?
When you throw a watch

**What did the scientist say
when she found bones
on the moon?**

'The cow didn't make it.'

**I'm reading an interesting
book on anti-gravity. I just
can't put it down!**

**What is the chemical
formula for water?**

HIJKLMNO

**What kind of weekend
breaks do nuclear
scientists like to go on?**

Fission trips

**What do you get when
a telescope runs into a
microscope?**

A collide-oscope

**I've got a device that lets me
collect futuristic herbs.
It's a thyme machine.**

What is a light year?

*The same as a regular year but
with less calories*

What did the scientist say
to the other scientist in an
argument?
'Let me atom!'

Why is a physics book always unhappy?
Because it always has lots of problems

What did one rocket scientist say to the other?
'I don't think you understand the gravity of the situation.'

How did the rocket lose its job?

It was fired

What are small scientists called?

Astro-gnomers

Knock, knock
Who's there?
A time traveller
A time traveller who?
Knock, knock

What did one astronomer say to the other?

'It's over your head.'

Did you know Einstein created a theory about space?

It was about time

What did the space scientist dress up as for Halloween?

FrankEinstein

Why isn't energy made of atoms?
It doesn't matter

How many astronomers does it take to change a light bulb?
None, astronomers aren't scared of the dark

Why can't you trust an atom?
They make up everything

That was a poor joke about infinity – it didn't have an ending

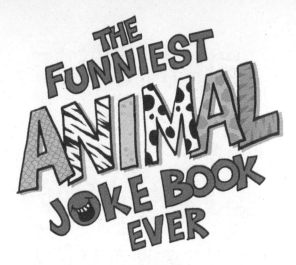

JOE KING

What do you call a pig who knows karate?
Pork chop

What is black, white and red all over?
A sunburnt penguin

What do you call an elephant in
a phone booth?
Stuck

You'll fall out of your tree
laughing at these rib-tickling
animal jokes!

9781783442331

Joe King

What's claret and blue and delicious? **A West Ham sandwich**

What did the ref say to the chicken who tripped a defender? **Fowl**

Why was the footballer upset on his birthday? **He got a red card**

These and many more howlers will make you laugh even if your team is losing!

9781849391115